MBUNDU

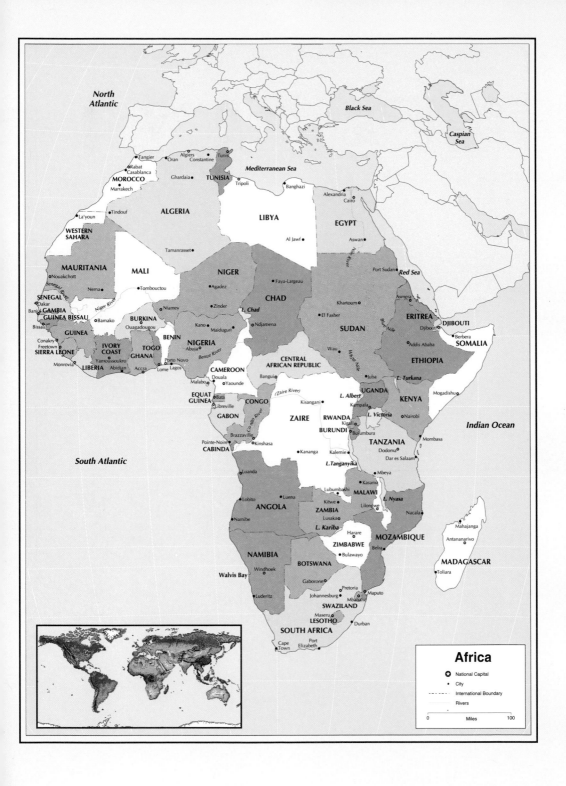

North
Atlantic

Black Sea

Caspian
Sea

Tangier
Algiers
Constantine
Tunis
Oran
TUNISIA
Mediterranean Sea
MOROCCO
Rabat
Casablanca
Ghardaia
Tripoli
Banghazi
Marrakech
Alexandria
Cairo
La'youn
Tindouf
EGYPT
WESTERN
SAHARA
ALGERIA
LIBYA
Aswan
Al Jawf

MAURITANIA
Nouakchott
MALI
NIGER
Port Sudan
Red Sea
Asmera
Nema
Agadez
Faya-Largeau
Tombouctou
CHAD
Khartoum
ERITREA
SENEGAL
Niger River
Zinder
Niamey
El Fasher
DJIBOUTI
Dakar
GAMBIA
SUDAN
Djibouti
Banjul
GUINEA BISSAU
BURKINA
Kano
Maiduguri
Berbera
Bamako
Ouagadougou
Ndjamena
SOMALIA
Bissau
Addis Ababa
GUINEA
BENIN
Wau
ETHIOPIA
Conakry
NIGERIA
Freetown
Abuja
White Nile
L. Turkana
SIERRA LEONE
IVORY
TOGO
Benue River
CENTRAL
COAST
GHANA
Porto Novo
AFRICAN REPUBLIC
Monrovia
Yamoussoukro
Lome Lagos
Juba
LIBERIA
Abidjan
Accra
CAMEROON
Bangui
UGANDA
KENYA
Douala
L. Albert
Malabo
Yaounde
Kisangani
Kampala
(Zaire River)
L. Victoria
Nairobi
EQUAT.
Bata
CONGO
Mogadishu
GUINEA
Libreville
ZAIRE
RWANDA
Indian Ocean
GABON
Kigali
Congo River
BURUNDI
Mombasa
Brazzaville
Kinshasa
Bujumbura
South Atlantic
Pointe-Noire
TANZANIA
Dodoma
CABINDA
Kananga
Kalemie
Dar es Salaam
L.Tanganyika
Luanda
Mbeya
Kasama
Lobito
Lubumbashi
MALAWI
L. Nyasa
Luena
Kitwe
Nacala
ANGOLA
ZAMBIA
Lilongwe
Namibe
Lusaka
Mahajanga
L. Kariba
MOZAMBIQUE
Harare
Antananarivo
ZIMBABWE
Beira
MADAGASCAR
NAMIBIA
Bulawayo
Windhoek
BOTSWANA
Toliara
Walvis Bay
Gaborone
Pretoria
Maputo
Johannesburg
Mbabane
Luderitz
SWAZILAND
Maseru
LESOTHO
Durban
SOUTH AFRICA
Cape
Port
Town
Elizabeth

Africa

⬡ National Capital

• City

-·-·-· International Boundary

——— Rivers

0   Miles   100

The Heritage Library of African Peoples

MBUNDU

Onwuka N. Njoku, Ph.D.

THE ROSEN PUBLISHING GROUP, INC.
NEW YORK

Published in 1997 by The Rosen Publishing Group, Inc.
29 East 21st Street, New York, NY 10010

First Edition

Manufactured in the United States of America

Library of Congress Cataloging-in-Publication Data

Njoku, Onwuka N.
  Mbundu / Onwuka N. Njoku. — 1st ed.
    p.   cm. — (The heritage library of African peoples)
  Includes bibliographical references and index.
  Summary: Discusses the history, culture, and daily life of the
Mbundu people of Angola.
  ISBN 0-8239-2004-6
  1. Mbundu (African people)—Juvenile literature.   [1. Mbundu
(African people)]   I. Title.   II. Series.
DT1308.M38N56   1996
967.3′00496399—dc20   96-32811
                                                                 CIP
                                                                  AC

Contents

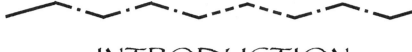

INTRODUCTION

THERE IS EVERY REASON FOR US TO KNOW something about Africa and to understand its past and the way of life of its peoples. Africa is a rich continent that has for centuries provided the world with art, culture, labor, wealth, and natural resources. It has vast mineral deposits, fossil fuels, and commercial crops.

But perhaps most important is the fact that fossil evidence indicates that human beings originated in Africa. The earliest traces of human beings and their tools are almost two million years old. Their descendants have migrated throughout the world. To be human is to be of African descent.

The experiences of the peoples who stayed in Africa are as rich and as diverse as of those who established themselves elsewhere. This series of books describes their environment, their modes of subsistence, their relationships, and their customs and beliefs. The books present the variety of languages, histories, cultures, and religions that are to be found on the African continent. They demonstrate the historical linkages between African peoples and the way contemporary Africa has been affected by European colonial rule.

Africa is large, complex, and diverse. It encompasses an area of more than 11,700,000 square miles. The United States, Europe, and India could fit easily into it. The sheer size is an indication of the continent's great variety in geography, terrain, climate, flora, fauna, peoples, languages, and cultures.

Much of contemporary Africa has been shaped by European colonial rule, industrialization, urbanization, and the demands of a world economic system. For more than seventy years, large regions of Africa were ruled by Great Britain, France, Belgium, Portugal, and Spain. African peoples from various ethnic, linguistic, and cultural backgrounds were brought together to form colonial states.

For decades Africans struggled to gain their independence. It was not until after World War II that the colonial territories become independent African states. Today, almost all of Africa is ruled by Africans. Large numbers of Africans live in modern cities. Rural Africa is also being transformed, and yet its people still engage in many of their age-old customs and beliefs.

Contemporary circumstances and natural events have not always been kind to ordinary Africans. Today, however, new popular social movements and technological innovations pose great promise for future development.

George C. Bond, Ph.D., Director
Institute of African Studies
Columbia University, New York

The Mbundu have a complex and vibrant culture. They have maintained their culture
throughout their long contact with European traders and colonists.
Here, an Mbundu man impersonates a lion ancestral spirit. Important ancestors are
associated with lions. This mask, made by the neighboring Chokwe people, is used
to protect Mbundu boys during their initiation.

1

THE LAND AND
THE PEOPLE

THE MBUNDU ARE ONE OF THE MOST ANCIENT peoples who live in the modern country of Angola. They have a proud history and a culture as rich and fascinating as those of better-known African societies.

The Mbundu live in an environment where droughts occur frequently, but they have found creative ways to deal with this problem. Over the centuries, the Mbundu have also had to adapt to numerous challenges.

Before the arrival of Europeans, the Mbundu had developed a strong and complex culture. Their political systems ran smoothly. Several Mbundu kingdoms rose to power and then declined. One of the most famous was the Ndongo Kingdom. It defeated a force of Portuguese invaders in the early 1500s.

The Mbundu have had much longer and more lasting contact with Europeans than

any other Angolan peoples—more than most
other African peoples. They have adopted certain aspects of Western culture without losing
their African roots. They have been able to
withstand great pressure from outsiders.
Throughout the first three centuries of Portuguese presence in Angola, it was mainly the
Mbundu people who had to deal with the problem of these Europeans.

The Mbundu are the largest ethnic group in
the modern state of Angola. They account for
more than one-third of Angola's population of
about 6.5 million people.

The Mbundu live in parts of northern and
central Angola. Most of their population lives in
the region of the Kwanza River.

The Mbundu are divided into subgroups or
kingdoms. These include the Lenge, the
Ndongo, the Songo, the Mbondo, the Hungu,
the Pende, the Imbangala, and the Libolo. Each
subg oup has unique characteristics.

The language of the Mbundu is Kimbundu.
It has two main dialects. The Akwaluanda
language, spoken around the city of Luanda
in the west, developed from the mixing of
Kimbundu-speakers and other Angolans in
Luanda. Ambakista, spoken in the east, devel-
oped along with the growth of a Portuguese-
Mbundu trading city, called Ambacca. These
Kimbundu dialects contain many Portuguese

CONGO

BRAZZAVILLE

Pointe-Noire

⊛ KINSHASA

Cabinda

Matadi

Congo R.

M'banza Congo

KONGO

Uíge

Caxito

MBUNDU

⊛ LUANDA

N'dalatando

Malanje

Cuango (Kwango) R.

PENDE

CHOKWE

LUNDA

HOLO

IMBANGALA

SONGO

OVIMBUNDU

Kikwit

Kananga

ZAIRE

Mwene Ditu

LUNDA

Lucapa

Saurimo

C H O K W E

Cuito R.

Kuito

Cuanza (Kwanza) R.

Cuvo R.

Sumbe

Luena

Kasai R.

Kasai R.

Lungué-Bungo R.

L W E N A

Zambezi R.

LUNDA

Kabompo R.

SOUTH

ATLANTIC

OCEAN

Lobito

Benguela

Huambo

Lubango

Namibe

C H O K W E

Cuando R.

Menongue

LUCHAZI

ZAMBIA

Mongu

Zambezi R.

Cunene (Kunenen) R.

Ondjiva

Cubango (Kubango) R.

Cuito R.

NAMIBIA

Sesfontein

Tsumeb

BOTSWANA

Maun

AFRICA

ANGOLA

The Mbundu are the largest ethnic group in Angola. Most of their population lives in the region of the Cuanza, or Kwanza, River.

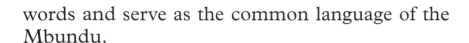

words and serve as the common language of the Mbundu.

▼ THE LAND ▼

The Mbundu live on a high plateau with numerous rivers. In Mbundu territories, rainfall is moderate in normal years. The rainy season in the north lasts from September to April; in the south, for shorter periods. It is difficult to tell when it will fall and how long the rainy season will last. As one moves south and west from the central highlands toward the Atlantic, the rainfall becomes less predictable. The coastal lowlands are extremely arid. Droughts have occured frequently in Angola from very early times. Long droughts have caused total crop failure and widespread famine. Local people dug reservoirs to catch floodwaters when the rains did come.

During droughts, plagues of locusts and other insects descend upon the crops and devour them. As if nature were at war with itself, periods of severe drought are often followed by equally destructive floods. This climate puts farming communities at risk and explains why there has traditionally been such an emphasis on rain in Mbundu politics and culture. One of the most important functions of Mbundu leaders was to use their spiritual powers to pray for good rains.

The climate and soil have largely determined

where the Mbundu live and how they farm. The moister and more fertile areas, especially river bottoms and mountain valleys, have attracted the greatest number of people. These areas include the plains along the Kunene and Kubango Rivers in the south and the middle section of the Kwango River.

The people raise fast-growing cereals such as sorghum and millet. Cassava, or manioc, imported from Brazil in the 1600s, is the main crop of the Mbundu north of the Kwanza River. Cassava roots are starchy—they look like sweet potatoes and are eaten in a similar way.

Iron ore is found both north and south of the Kwanza River. Salt, essential for human survival, was produced from seawater. The salty marshes of the interior, especially in the region of the Mbundu kingdom of Libolo, were also used for saltmaking.

▼ ORIGINS ▼

The origins of the Mbundu are uncertain. The Portuguese, who established contact with the Mbundu in the late 1400s, had little or no interest in the people's history. The Portuguese left few written descriptions of the Mbundu. For this reason, there are many gaps in our knowledge of Mbundu history.

The Mbundu have three versions of their early history. Similar in some respects, these versions also differ from each other. They have all been passed from generation to generation by word of mouth. Such histories are called "oral histories."

One version says that the ancestors of the Mbundu originally came from "the great water," which is believed to be the Atlantic Ocean. Historians of the Mbundu have identified the island of Luanda as their place of origin.

The five main Mbundu ancestors named in this version are Kajinga ka Mbulu, who is said to have founded the Mbondo Kingdom; Matamba a Mbulu, ancestor of the Lenge; Mbunda a Mulu, mother of the Pende; Kongo dya Mbulu, who gave rise to the Hungu; and Zundu dya Mbulu, mother of the Ndongo.

These ancestors are said to have introduced the Mbundu symbol of authority called the *lunga* (plural: *malunga*). The *lunga* is a sacred object in the shape of a human figure carved in wood. Many Mbundu groups have *malunga*. The *lunga* is used to bring rain and it is linked to the success of farming, which was the main activity of the Mbundu in the past.

The second version, which was written down in the 1600s, says that the Mbundu once lived in several independent chiefdoms. In the early days, it is said, the Mbundu led a simple life and used only stone and wood for tools and weapons. Eventually a blacksmith called Mussuri rose to power by bartering iron goods for food. Through both his trading and ironworking skills, Mussuri eventually became king. Mussuri married a woman called Ngola Inene. Ngola Inene had a daughter, Samba, whose children founded several peoples: the Ndongo, the Hungu, the Pende, the Lenge, the Mbondo, the Imbangala, the Songo, and the Libolo.

It is thought that the most complete version of early Mbundu history is the one told by the Pende people. After leaving their original settlement in the 1600s, the Pende settled along the Kasai River. There they were shielded from Western contact until the 1800s. In about 1950, a Pende historian who came from a family of chiefs recited the following version of Mbundu origins.

The earliest ancestor of the Mbundu, Ngola Kilaji, lived at Tandji in Milumbu, a region near the upper Zambezi River. Ngola's people were hunters and warriors. They had no

Ancestors are a very important part of Mbundu culture. They play a key role in bringing rain. Seen here is a wood carving of a female ancestral figure; her flame-shaped cap suggests that she is a member of a ruling family.

knowledge of iron but used wooden and stone weapons. One day Ngola migrated west with his people toward the sea. Along the route, Ngola left groups of men at strategic places, where they founded villages, *jingundu* (singular: *ngundu*). When Ngola reached the Kwanza River, he followed its course down to Luanda on the coast.

For a long time, Ngola settled on the Luanda plains. There he was joined by a group of people led by Bembo Kalamba, a blacksmith. Ngola learned ironworking, pottery, and weaving from Bembo Kalamba and his people. Kalamba's wife, Ngombe dia Nganda, taught Ngola's people farming and cattle-raising. The followers of Ngola married the daughters of Ngombe, who became the mothers of the Mbundu subgroups. Together they lived happily and in prosperity on the plains of Luanda.

One day, the Europeans arrived and drove Ngola away with guns. But by then Ngola had founded the kingdom of Ndongo. He had also introduced an authority symbol known as *ngola* (plural: *angola*), from which the modern state of Angola received its name. The *ngola* symbol, made of iron, is widely used by Mbundu peoples today.▲

2

EARLY HISTORY AND CULTURE

FROM VERY EARLY IN THEIR HISTORY, THE Mbundu have lived in several independent villages. Each village managed its own land and water and shared these resources.

The Mbundu are a matrilineal people, meaning that one's family line, or lineage, is traced through the mother's line of descent. However, political authority was controlled mostly by men.

In the Mbundu view, women continue the family line by giving birth. Thus, the Mbundu emphasize the role of women in childbearing. They celebrate the first menstruation of young girls as evidence of their readiness to bear children.

The Mbundu showed their respect for family ancestors through special ceremonies. The village head was responsible for communicating between humans and spirits. He was expected to

In rural Mbundu villages, building a house usually involves many members of the village. Seen here is a group of men adding the thatched roof to a house built of sun-dried brick.

provide village members with land and to persuade rain to fall at the right time and in the right amount.

The village was the center of the social and political life of the Mbundu. Each village consisted mainly of people from the same family, or lineage. The oldest man was usually the head of both the village and the lineage.

The village-lineage defined the individual's place in the society. If there was no lineage (*ngundu*), there would be no relatives to call on for help, no right to marry, and no right to grow food. No individual could survive without the help of his or her *ngundu* (plural: *jingundu*). Not surprisingly, people were extremely loyal to their lineages.

The Mbundu placed great importance on their *jingundu* and kept them intact through the centuries.

The strength of Mbundu village-lineages can be seen in their ability to adapt to changing circumstances while retaining their independence. Communities were able both to expand their territory and to form a more centralized society. They did this without losing their own culture and sense of unity.

▼ CROSS-LINEAGE LINKS ▼

The Mbundu also have customs that create links between different lineages. Most important is the fact that people marry into lineages other than their own.

Professionals such as diviners, healers, and hunters also crossed lineage boundaries, because they could be apprenticed to masters from any lineage.

After training, the apprentices underwent an initiation ceremony attended by their local masters. When a master hunter died, all members of the association from the surrounding areas gathered for his burial. They also organized a communal hunt in his honor. Such events created unity between professionals. The masters were able to travel far beyond their own village-lineages and meet their neighboring colleagues.

Mbundu neighborhoods held regular circum-

During initiation, Mbundu boys spend months in secret camps, making the transition from boyhood to adulthood under the supervision of elders. The Chokwe, neighbors of the Mbundu, have similar initiation traditions. Seen here is a Chokwe youth at his graduation ceremony, wearing the traditional body paint, fiber skirt, and a hat that resembles those worn by Portuguese officers during colonial times.

cision camps for young men from the region.
Men from different lineages were brought
together and went through the same ceremonies.

All these practices created ties across village-
lineage boundaries and blurred the distinctions
between relatives and nonrelatives.

▼ AUTHORITY ▼

Mbundu officeholders ruled through their
possession of sacred objects like the *lunga* and
ngola, which were handed down from their
predecessors. Through these symbols, chiefs
could call upon supernatural powers. Both
chiefship and kingship were thus sacred among
the Mbundu. Leaders were treated with great
respect and were surrounded by many taboos, or
special rules of behavior.

As leaders took on new powers, or because of
changing circumstances and needs, later genera-
tions of leaders introduced new symbols. Par-
ticular symbols therefore came to be associated
with different historical periods.

▼ *LUNGA* KINGS ▼

The introduction of the wooden *lunga* symbol
by the Pende marks the moment when the
Mbundu first tried to expand their borders. The
holder of the *lunga* knew how to please the
Mbundu ancestor spirits. He claimed authority
over anyone who lived on the land of the

ancestors. Unlike the previous system in which power was passed from father to son in the same lineage, this system was tied to an actual region.

Pende *lunga* kings extended their authority across the plateau that lies to the north and west of Luanda. They brought under their control many village-lineages. One of the most powerful Pende kings was Batatu a Kuhongo, whose territory was in the region of the Kwango River.

The source of the *lunga* kings' power was their control over the salt deposits of their region. The *lunga* kings took control of the salt trade routes, but were over-powered in the early 1500s by the expanding state of Matamba.

▼ *NGOLA* KINGS ▼

The introduction of iron had a great impact on Mbundu history. According to Mbundu oral history, the blacksmith king Ngola Mussuri is thought to have introduced ironworking skills. These enabled the Mbundu to make iron tools and weapons such as axes, machetes, arrowheads, and spears. These were vastly superior to earlier

Mbundu rulers historically owned sacred items that possessed supernatural powers and served as symbols of their authority. Carved along the top of this Songo pipe are dogs, which are considered protective creatures by the Mbundu, and a chief talking to another man.

stone and wooden tools. Ngola kings from the
1450s to the 1550s kept an iron bracelet as their
lineage symbol.

Ngola leaders expanded their chiefdoms and
brought many lineages under their control
through their control of iron. In this way, they
turned the *ngola* from a lineage symbol into the
basis of an enlarged state or kingdom. When an
Mbundu lineage received an *ngola*, it appointed
a guardian for it. They believed that the symbol
gave him access to special spiritual forces that
were necessary for controlling human affairs.

The most famous *ngola* kingdom was the
Ndongo. It lay just south of the powerful Kongo
Kingdom in what is now Zaire. The two kingdoms were in constant competition with each
other. The Ndongo first introduced iron to the
region. The Ndongo Kingdom is said to have
begun well before 1500 as a small state north of
the Kwanza River. In time, it developed into a
regional center. Its society consisted of many
different ranks. The village chief was at the low-
est level of the complex administration.

We do not know exactly how the Mbundu
first developed kingdoms. Chiefs and kings were
first the guardians of rain-making shrines. By the
1300s these spiritual guardians had become
chiefs who demanded to be honored and paid
by the people. During famines, they distributed
food to their "subjects." They also protected

them from attacks from other groups and relocated their villages during droughts. Over time, these leaders combined religious and non-religious duties.

In the case of the Ndongo, oral history states that the guardians of the shrines were also expert ironworkers. By 1500 a king called Ngola Kilaji ruled all Ndongo territory. By the time the Portuguese arrived in Mbundu territory, the *ngola* kings had overtaken most of the *lunga* kings.

▼ LIBOLO KINGSHIP ▼

The Mbundu never came under one single kingdom. The Libolo Kingdom covered the northern territory of the Mbundu and had a clearer center of control than any other Mbundu kingdom.

Libolo rulers did not inherit their titles through their family line. Rather, they appointed kings by giving them titles called *mavunga* (*vunga*: singular). Titles were awarded for obedience and allegiance to the king.

The power of the Libolo peaked before the mid-1500s and then declined. Libolo kings, the *hango*, ruled through provincial governors. The governors received their *mavunga* symbols from the king, who gave them their titles.

Each Mbundu state showed its difference from its predecessor by adopting one or more new symbols and reducing the roles of earlier power symbols. By doing this, ruling lineages were able to adapt to changes and expand their power and control.▲

chapter

3

THE ECONOMY

PRECOLONIAL AFRICAN ECONOMIES WERE much more complex than most people realize. The economy of the Mbundu had three main parts: farming, manufacturing, and trade. These were so closely connected that the health of one affected that of the others. Farming combined the tasks of growing crops and keeping animals. Hunting and fishing were also important.

▼ FARMING ▼

Farming was the central activity of every Mbundu man, woman, and child.

The climate determined when crops could be planted and harvested. Farmers practiced slash-and-burn agriculture. First they cleared the farmland by chopping growth with machetes and then burned the land before the rains came. Because of the uncertainty of rains, the entire

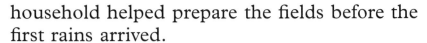

household helped prepare the fields before the first rains arrived.

The main crops for the Mbundu people were sorghum and millet. Each family harvested and stored enough food to eat until the next harvest. Surplus crops were traded for other items such as tobacco, meat, beeswax, and tools. Until the Portuguese introduced cassava from South America, the Mbundu had no drought-resistant crops. Successful farming depended on taking advantage of the rainy season to grow enough food to last through the dry months.

Goats and sheep were raised in most areas. Cattle did well on the higher land south of the Kwanza River. Cattle provided meat, milk, and leather. Mbundu cattle herders drove their animals to higher ground during the rains, and then down the hills during the dry months. This practice is known as transhumance.

▼ HUNTING ▼

In addition to grains, the Mbundu ate wild vegetables and fruits gathered by women and children, and game hunted by men. These other foods were especially important during the dry months when vegetation was scarce. Professional hunters were highly respected in the community. They used iron-tipped arrows, machetes, spears, traps, and nets to hunt. The game included

During the rainy season, Mbundu women spend long hours farming their fields and growing grains and other crops to feed their families. This woman is cleaning millet grain by tossing it in a basket.

rats, birds, porcupines, grazing animals, hyenas, lions, and even elephants.

A hunter who killed a powerful animal such as a lion was given special recognition in his community. The fangs, claws, and skin of the lion were used by medicine men to make charms. Its skin was also used for making skin bags and for decorating royal palaces. Elephants provided ivory, a very precious trade item.

The dry months were best for fishing, because as the water levels dropped, fish became trapped in shallow pools.

Mbundu men and women take advantage of the rainy season by growing enough crops to last them through the dry months. This Mbundu man displays some of his crops grown during the rainy season, among which are bananas, sugar cane, and pineapples.

▼ CRAFTS ▼

Mbundu men made nets for fishing and hunting. They also wove baskets, mats, and hats from grass. Pestles, mortars, and seats were carved from wood. In river areas men made dugout canoes.

Clay pottery was the specialty of women. Mothers taught their daughters the art of making pottery. The earthenwares were used to carry and store water and grain, as dishes, and for ceremonies.

Ironworking is one of the most important professions among the Mbundu, as blacksmiths create everything from kitchenwares to weapons. Seen here is a blacksmith at work.

▼ BLACKSMITHS ▼

Apart from farming, the most important work was ironworking. Farmers needed hoes, machetes, and digging tools. Hunters needed arrows, spears, and hunting bells, and fishermen needed harpoons. Woodworkers needed axes, carving knives, and scrapers. Domestic utensils such as kitchen knives were also supplied by the blacksmith. Iron weapons were used in wars. Those groups with more advanced weapons were able to defeat their rivals and expand their kingdoms.

Blacksmiths also produced items of cultural and social value. These included royal symbols, bells and gongs for ceremonies, and ornaments such as rings, pendants, and bangles. Blacksmiths were widely respected in their communities.

Blacksmiths were also believed to possess great spiritual powers. Throughout much of ancient Africa, iron was believed to have special powers. Except for those specially trained, iron was very dangerous. Properly handled, iron could bring about many blessings; mishandled, it could bring bad consequences to the community. For these reasons, the blacksmith was viewed with awe.

Blacksmiths found many ways to emphasize their importance and protect their profession. The skill was made hereditary, passed from father to son. Training involved a long and difficult apprenticeship that ended in an elaborate ceremony. Entry into the profession was controlled by a strict guild of master smiths. Every major step in the process of producing iron required special religious ceremonies.

In some Mbundu kingdoms, salt resources were controlled by royal agents. These agents made sure that local producers promptly paid a share of their salt to the king. Saltwater was filtered and then boiled over a low fire to produce salt crystals that were then made into balls and cones. These were used for trade and as a form of currency.

▼ MEDICINE ▼

Traditional medicine men provided medical and health services to the public. They knew

how to use herbs, leaves, barks, and roots of
trees to treat illnesses. They treated numerous
diseases, such as dysentery, sleeping sickness,
diarrhea, and yellow fever. Some specialized in
setting broken bones; others, very often women,
specialized in the health of women and babies.
In the West today, traditional African medicine is
increasingly being recognized for its ability to
heal both physical and psychological problems.
Many people in Africa and elsewhere are calling
for more mixing between the two traditions.

▼ TRADE ▼

Trade was vital to the Mbundu economy,
because no Mbundu community was self-
sufficient. The uneven distribution of resources
meant that some communities produced certain
goods in abundance but lacked others.

Iron technology helped the Mbundu to work
more efficiently in their environment. It also
encouraged people to become specialists in par-
ticular kinds of work. People who made crafts
such as pottery or wood carvings traded their
products with farmers, fishermen, and hunters.

Each region became skilled at certain tasks
and produced its own items for trade. This
regional specialization led to trade between
regions. Increasing competition for scarce resources sometimes forced village chiefdoms
to join together with their neighbors and form

Angola has long been a center for trade between African groups, and also between Africans and Europeans. Seen here is a wooden figurine of a man riding an ox, historically one of the primary means of transportation for Mbundu traders along Angolan trade routes.

larger states. The population grew and more land was used for farming. Portuguese priests who visited Angola in the 1500s described the country as rich and densely populated.

Iron products and salt were the most widely traded products in the Mbundu hinterland. Salt was used as a form of currency on both sides of the Kwanza River as late as the 1700s.

Dried fish came from the coastal region of Luanda and rivers in the hinterland. To communities living far from the rivers and lakes, dried fish was a desirable rarity.

Ivory and copper, in the form of bracelets, rings, and necklaces, came from the Kongo Kingdom north of the Mbundu. The forest area of the Kongo Kingdom also produced a beautiful kind of textile, known as raffia cloth, which was woven from palm leaves.

The trading network covered a wide area and linked the Mbundu with neighboring lands.

One trade route ran from the Ovimbundu territories in the south, northward through the Kassanje Kingdom of the Imbangala into the Kongo Kingdom. Ovimbundu traders brought iron products as well as livestock.

Another route went eastward from Luanda on the coast via Mbundu, Kassanje, and Musumba (capital of the Lunda empire in Zaire), to the kingdom of Kazembe in Zambia. At Musumba, the route branched northwest to the Kuba on the edge of the Zairean forest. Copper and fish were the most important products from this area.

The Mbundu played the role of middlemen in the movement of goods between the coastal areas and the hinterland.▲

chapter

4

THE PORTUGUESE AND THE MBUNDU

THE PORTUGUESE LANDED AT THE MOUTH OF
the Congo River in 1483. They established trade
and diplomatic relations with the Mani Kongo,
ruler of the Kongo Kingdom. At first, the main
export of the Kongo Kingdom was ivory. Raffia
cloth was also bought by Portuguese traders and
exported to other coastal Africans. In return, the
Portuguese sold fabrics, rum, tobacco, and guns
to the Kongo people.

Later the Portuguese established sugar plantations on the islands of Principe and Sáo Tomé
off the west coast of Africa. They also established large plantations and mines in Brazil,
South America. A large number of laborers were
needed to work the mines and plantations. This
caused the Portuguese to look for slave labor.

Slaves became the main export item from the
Kongo Kingdom. To extend their search for

slaves south of Kongo territory, the Portuguese established a base at what is today the port of Luanda.

Apart from trading in slaves, the Portuguese had two other commercial goals in Angola. They believed that the hinterland was rich in precious minerals, especially silver. They also hoped to set up large plantations on the region's fertile land.

The Portuguese mission in Angola inevitably brought them into direct conflict with the local peoples, whose political and economic life they disrupted. From this time on, Angolan people resisted the Portuguese. The Mbundu kingdom of Ndongo bore the brunt of Portuguese attacks, which lasted for centuries.

The Portuguese dream of mining precious minerals was not realized as none could be found. Their attempt to establish plantations achieved little success, thanks to the stiff resistance of the Ndongo Kingdom. Indeed, in one of their first major military invasions into the central Luanda Plateau, the powerful Portuguese force was defeated by the Ndongo army.

▼ SLAVE TRADE ▼

The Portuguese continued regular slave trade and slave raids. The central Luanda Plateau, home of the Mbundu people, became the main target. In 1557 Ngola Inene, king of Ndongo, attempted to find a diplomatic solution to the

The Mbundu are the dominant ethnic group in Luanda, the capital of Angola. Seen here is the urban port of Luanda, where many Mbundu now move to find jobs in modern Angola's economy.

Portuguese slave raids. The king sent diplomats to Lisbon to ask Queen Catherine to set up a Portuguese embassy in his capital. Instead she sent a mission of Jesuit priests. For a while, Portuguese-Mbundu relations improved, but not for long.

In 1571 the Portuguese crown granted a royal charter to permit a Portuguese named Paulo Dias to colonize Angola at his own expense. Dias thought that the charter gave him the authority to raid for slaves and loot the wealth of the Angolan people. Through a series of military expeditions, the Portuguese extended their foothold from the area around Luanda eastward into the heartland of the Mbundu. As they advanced, they established

Portuguese slave traders established a fort at what is today the port of Luanda, partly to serve as a holding area for slaves. Today the fort (above) houses a military museum.

forts and stationed soldier-traders to staff them.

Finally in 1618 the Portuguese achieved their goal. With the assistance of the Imbangala, a mobile, warlike group, the Portuguese sacked the Ndongo capital, looted the royal court, and executed many nobles. The king sought refuge on an island in the Kwanza River. So ended the proud Ndongo dynasty.

Portuguese advances inland and increased slave raiding created insecurity among Angolan communities. The Portuguese forced conquered African kingdoms to pay tribute in slaves. Increasingly, slave export became the most important part of the Mbundu economy. By the 1750s Luanda had become one of the busiest slave ports on the African Atlantic coast. Estimates of slave exports from Angola during the period vary from 5,000 to 10,000 per year, the majority of whom were Mbundu. This had a devastating effect on the Mbundu, whose population was only around 500,000. The slaves were mostly men and women under thirty years old. The slave trade robbed the society of its strongest adults, ruined the economy, and weakened the people's ability to defend themselves.

▼ QUEEN NZINGA ▼

The collapse of the Ndongo dynasty led to the rise of a remarkable ruler, Queen Nzinga. She dominated the political scene in Angola for nearly half a century. She realized the hopelessness of organizing a military campaign against the Portuguese. Nzinga chose a diplomatic solution instead.

To establish her policy, Queen Nzinga personally went to offer peace to the Portuguese governor at Luanda in 1623. Portugal recognized Nzinga's authority over her kingdom. She returned to her kingdom after having been baptized and given the Christian name of Dona Ana de Souza. The Governor of Luanda became her godfather. Portuguese-Ndongo relations were better than ever before.

With Portuguese assistance, Nzinga ousted bands of Imbangala warriors who had terrorized her kingdom and made the trade routes unsafe. But this did not bring peace to Queen Nzinga, for the Portuguese continued to raid her kingdom for slaves and precious items. Queen Nzinga was forced to flee and resettle in

Matamba, beyond the reach of the Portuguese.

The Portuguese installed a new Ndongo king who would enforce their policies: King Ari Kiluanje. His subjects thought that he lacked traditional authority and believed him incapable of playing the spiritual role essential for a Mbundu ruler. Meanwhile Nzinga gradually built up a powerful kingdom in Matamba. She trained a mighty army and stirred people's distrust of Ari Kiluanje. She led her troups in battle against the hated ruler. From the mid-1620s to the 1630s, war raged in Kiluanje's kingdom.

In 1641 the Dutch captured Luanda. Nzinga allied with the Dutch, but the Portuguese eventually recaptured Luanda and expelled the Dutch from Angola. Nzinga arranged a peace and retreated back to Matamba.

Nzinga built Matamba into an important commercial kingdom. Portuguese traders (*pombeiros*) assembled at Matamba to exchange European products for slaves. The Portuguese governor of Luanda sent an official to regulate trade between the *pombeiros* and African traders. By the time Nzinga died in 1663, Matamba was a flourishing kingdom in its own right.▲

Queen Nzinga was a remarkable Mbundu ruler who lived in the 1600s. She tried to make peace with Portuguese colonists through diplomatic means. Seen here is an historical portrait of Queen Nzinga.

chapter

5

ROAD TO INDEPENDENCE

IN THE 1880S EUROPEAN POWERS BEGAN TO divide Africa among themselves without regard for what the Africans thought. At the Berlin Conference in 1884–1885, the European powers decided to give Portugal the power to colonize Angola because of its long presence there. Among Portugal's other African colonies were Mozambique, Guinea-Bissau, and Cape Verde.

In the 1890s the Portuguese colonial government established trade taxes and regulations, called tariffs, in Angola. This meant that Angolans could not sell their exports freely, nor could they buy from the cheapest suppliers of manufactured products. They had to sell to, and buy from, Portugal. Many factories in Portugal were reorganized to produce goods for the Angolan market. By 1898 the slave trade had been officially outlawed. Nevertheless, it continued illegally, although it declined steadily.

A rubber boom occurred in Europe and America in the 1890s. Mbundu farmers began collecting wild rubber, which was bringing good prices. This opportunity enabled Mbundu slave traders to change their occupation to a legal form of trade. The boom brought an influx of Portuguese immigrants to Angola, and especially to Mbundu country. The white population in Angola rose from 3,000 in the 1860s to 13,000 at the turn of the twentieth century.

The rubber boom collapsed within the first decade of the twentieth century. The market for coffee however began to flourish. Mbundu farmers who had been collecting and selling wild coffee stepped up their efforts. Coffee brought more waves of Portuguese immigrants to Angola, their number reaching 170,000 by 1959. As these immigrants poured in, vast acres of the most fertile land were taken from the local people to give to settlers. By the 1950s, the fertile Mbundu land had been turned into the largest coffee plantations in the world. Thousands of Mbundu farmers were displaced.

Because the working conditions on the white-owned plantations were extremely harsh and the wages were incredibly low, workers were in short supply. New administrative measures were put in place to force black Africans to work for the

Throughout history a variety of different products have drawn both Europeans and rural Angolans to the coastal urban centers. Seen here are a group of rural Mbundu men looking for work at Moçamedes, a port city in Angola.

white owners. Dispossessed African landowners could be declared illegal wanderers and then forced into wage jobs as laborers on the land that had once belonged to them.

In the Kwanza and Kwango River basins, Mbundu farmers were forced by the Portuguese government to plant cotton, but they were paid less than fair market value for their cotton. They were forbidden to give first priority to growing food for themselves, so the policy caused severe food shortages. But the Portuguese government under the dictatorship of Antonio Salázar claimed that reports of famines were a figment of black imagination.

The loss of land, compulsory cotton farming, harsh and unfair labor conditions, low prices, and delayed payment became sources of conflict between the Mbundu and the white plantation owners. The Mbundu district of north central Angola witnessed two major rebellions, in 1913 and in 1917–18. Cottonseed was burned, European stores were attacked, river barges were sunk, and cattle were killed. The colonial government responded with great ruthlessness. Thousands of Mbundu farmers were killed, their homes destroyed, and their crops looted and burned in order to destroy anything of value.

Most Portuguese immigrants were poor and illiterate criminals and desperados. They dreamed of an El Dorado (a land of prosperity) in Angola. A handful of them realized this dream, but the overwhelming majority remained poor. They competed with black Angolans for jobs such as carpenters, drivers, mechanics, hotel porters, hawkers, shop assistants, cleaners, and prostitutes. They often felt hostile toward the Africans with whom they competed. However, the competition was unequal, for the whites were favored over better-qualified and more experienced black Angolans.

▼ LIBERATION STRUGGLE ▼
Elsewhere in Africa, colonial powers were forced by African demands to give independence to their African colonies in the 1950s. But Portugal was not prepared to free its African colonies.

Labor exploitation and job competition have long been sources of conflict between the Mbundu and European colonists. Seen here are Mbundu dock workers at Moçamedes.

The Portuguese viewed colonialism as a permanent arrangement. In 1951 Lisbon converted its African colonies into "overseas Portugal." Calls for African independence were violently repressed.

Faced with the firm attitude of Portugal, African nationalists in Angola, as in Guinea-Bissau and Mozambique, reluctantly adopted a revolutionary philosophy. In 1956 Agostino Neto formed a liberation movement called the Movement for the Popular Liberation of Angola (MPLA). This was followed by two other liberation movements—the Front for the National Liberation of Angola (FNLA) and its breakaway group, the Union for Total Independence of Angola (UNITA).

MPLA was the leading movement. It drew its

support mostly from the Kimbundu-speaking people. FNLA drew its support mostly from the Kikongo-speaking people in the north, while UNITA drew its support from the Ovimbundu in the south.

The formation of these armed liberation movements marked the onset of a long and bitterly fought war against the Portuguese. By 1960 the Portuguese had thrown most MPLA leaders into jail without fair trials. In January 1961, desperation and despair, made worse by low prices for cotton and delayed payments, drove black farmers to open violence.

The resistance was swiftly crushed, but not before it spread to urban Luanda. There two unsuccessful attempts to free the nationalist leaders were made on the prisons. Panic-stricken whites quickly formed armed vigilante gangs. They swept through black slums in a massacre that claimed many lives. Tens of thousands of Angolan refugees streamed into Zaire and Zambia.

Such repressive measures failed to crush Africans' determination to be free. Africans who had been robbed of their land, deserters from the colonial army, fugitives, and the urban poor joined the liberation movements, swelling their ranks. If colonial authorities suspected Mbundu villages of harboring guerrilla fighters, such villages were forcefully relocated in cramped areas that were fenced in with barbed wire and guarded. The economic impact of such actions was devastating.

In 1961 people generally assumed that the war would be over within a year, but it dragged on for thirteen more. The Portuguese army was at war with all its African colonies. By 1974 the Portuguese army was convinced that it could not win these wars. Political settlement with the liberation movements was the only way out. On April 25, 1974, the government of Portugal was overthrown by the Portuguese military. These new military leaders wanted to then negotiate with the liberation fighters and pull out of Angola.

In 1975, with the help of President Jomo Kenyatta of Kenya, the Portuguese tried to create a government for Angola that included representatives from the three liberation movements. However, MPLA, FNLA, and UNITA began to fight among themselves for control. The MPLA, the oldest and most popular liberation movement among rural people, particularly the Mbundu, gained control of Luanda.

Angolan independence was scheduled for November 1975, and MPLA expected to take power. On November 11, 1975, the Portuguese pulled out of Angola. They did not hand over power to any of the liberation movements but to "the Angolan people." Neto, on behalf of MPLA, declared Angola independent.

Some foreign powers did not want to see the socialist MPLA come to power. Zairean and FNLA forces, armed and backed by the United States, attacked MPLA government forces from the north. UNITA, along with South African forces, invaded from the south. With the aid of a Soviet-equipped Cuban force, Neto's MPLA government drove the rebels back.

A peace was arranged, and the MPLA won elections that were held in 1992, but UNITA rejected the results. Fighting continued until June 1993, when the rebels finally signed an agreement with the MPLA government. However, after nearly twenty years of war, the political situation in Angola remains fragile.▲

chapter

6

CONTINUITY AND CHANGE

THE 600 YEARS OF EUROPEAN PRESENCE IN
Angola have greatly influenced various aspects of
Angolan lives. Not all parts of Angola have been
equally affected. In general, Western impact has
been strongest in the urban areas.

The Kimbundu-speaking people were the first
Angolans to have contact with the Portuguese.
They are also the dominant ethnic group in the
capital city of Luanda. For these reasons, the
Mbundu have experienced Portuguese influence
longer and more intensely than other native
Angolans. This influence is noticeable in their
political, social, economic, and cultural lives.

▼ POLITICAL ▼

The Mbundu have lost their independence
and have come under the political control of the
nation-state of Angola, which contains many
non-Kimbundu-speaking peoples. Since the

colonial era, the center of political control has been Luanda. However, the colonial authorities had needed the support of traditional village and district heads. This helped to preserve the traditional Mbundu institution of *ngundu*.

Today the MPLA controls a strong central government with weak political authorities at lower levels. National unity is emphasized by the central government. Angola is divided into 80 provinces and 161 districts. The districts are further divided into communes, quarters, and villages. Local peoples' assemblies operate at these various administrative levels. Education and loyalty to the MPLA are the chief requirements for election.

Party members join together to form small groups. Today the building block of society consists of people who support the MPLA party, rather than people from the same lineage (as in the past). As a result, the authority of Mbundu lineage elders has greatly diminished. All the same, *ngundu* remains a key institution in the lives of the Mbundu, especially rural people. Village heads are still the guardians of the people's traditions. They ensure that traditional festivals are held and settle disputes between members of their *ngundu*.

▼ ECONOMIC ▼
Under the Portuguese, the traditional

Mbundu economy was greatly changed and damaged. Many Mbundu farmers lost their land and were forced into farm labor. Others were forced to produce cash crops. Only areas that produced export crops received colonial attention. As a result of these new uses for land, subsistence farming declined.

Today, however, the system of traditional Mbundu farming continues to focus on the family as workers. Women still bear the brunt of the workload. Today the already weak soil is worsening as more and more people work it, using the age-old slash-and-burn farming system. Today blacksmiths are no longer the main suppliers of work tools; these are imported. The head of the lineage is still expected to ensure good harvests by praying for the rains to come when required.

Since independence, Mbundu farmers can now work their own land again. Their lands are no longer taken away. Guarded villages no longer exist in Mbundu society. The MPLA government has encouraged the formation of farming cooperatives in which Mbundu farmers work together and share profits. However, most farmers still work individually on their land and produce most of the food they consume. Increasingly, rural farmers now produce surpluses for the urban and world markets.

The Mbundu have successfully combined

new crops with traditional ones, thereby increasing their food supply. Corn and cassava have become staples among the Mbundu. However, the risk of crop failure is still a threat.

Urban-dwelling Mbundu are dependent on wage-earning jobs. Unemployment is high. Those who have jobs work in the modern sector of the economy, such as factories and service industries. Some are civil servants for the government. Most of these people are very poorly paid. Many live in makeshift and over-crowded huts in city slums where there are many social problems.

Colonialism tended to

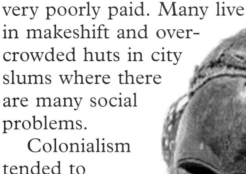

Mbundu village leaders still ensure that traditional festivals and ceremonies are followed today. Seen here is a mask that represents an ancient female ancestor.

sideline women in Angolan society. The MPLA government has pursued a policy of female equality. Women are now encouraged to go to school. They hold jobs that were once assumed to belong only to men. Some Mbundu women serve as road sweepers, traffic controllers, doctors, and even ministers.

▼ CHRISTIANITY ▼

Christianity has caused deep changes in traditional Mbundu society. Christian missionaries have been active since the 1500s. Backed by the Portuguese government the Roman Catholic Church was the driving force behind the Portuguese invasion. In 1940 an agreement was made between the Pope and Portugal. Under the plan, all missionaries in Angola had to be Portuguese except where severe shortages required others to be brought in. The idea was to use the Catholic Church to spread the influence of Portuguese culture.

Missionaries introduced a new religion that challenged Mbundu ancestor worship and the belief in spirit forces and inanimate objects. Christians condemned the customs of polygyny, which allowed men to have more than one wife; initiation ceremonies; and other practices. They preached absolute obedience to authority, meaning that the Mbundu should obey the Portuguese authorities. They urged the people to

discard the ways of their fathers and become
Christian to save their souls.

Over the years, a great number of Mbundu
people have become Christians, especially in the
urban centers. Many have replaced their
Mbundu names with Christian or biblical ones.
Some Mbundu have been more interested in the
benefits of being Christian—such as better education and job opportunities—than in Christianity's actual message. In everyday life, many
Mbundu Christians struggle with the conflicts
between the new religion and the religion of
their ancestors.

Millions of Mbundu people have held on to
their earlier religious beliefs and customs. These
people still honor their ancestors and worship
the spirits of such elements as the water, the
hills, and the forests. As in earlier times, the
traditional Mbundu still believe that all evil,
including death, has both physical and spiritual
causes. A man might die of a snakebite, but it
is the power of evil that kills him. Floods,
droughts, and epidemics are not simply natural
phenomena; they are the punishments of
angry spirits who then need to be calmed.

In the civil war in Angola, many Mbundu
fighters consulted diviners who gave them
potions believed to make their bodies bullet-
proof. Many Mbundu and non-Mbundu are
known to pay regular visits to traditional

diviners. The colonial authorities condemned those Portuguese immigrants who took part in powerful Mbundu ceremonies and other religious activities.

▼ ASSIMILATION ▼

The main policy of the Portuguese administration in Angola was assimilation, that is, bringing Angolan Africans under Portuguese control by making them absorb the foreign culture. Colonial education was one of the most powerful tools the Portuguese used to achieve their goal.

The missionaries were the providers of colonial education, and so Christianity and education went hand in hand. The missionaries established schools in various parts of Angola under the strict supervision of the colonial state. The Christian missions made regular reports about their work to the colonial authorities.

Several mission schools were established in Mbundu country. The language of instruction was Portuguese, and Kimbundu was forbidden. The classes contained few or no themes relevant to the local people. Portuguese culture and civilization were praised while indigenous culture was looked down upon. The idea was to make the local people believe that the Portuguese culture was the way to the future. Such schools were useful in achieving the colonial goals,

Many Mbundu still pay regular visits to traditional diviners and spiritualists. Here, a diviner holds in his hand a small antelope horn that, depending on which direction it points, will give either a negative or affirmative answer to his client's questions.

because students were taught these notions at impressionable ages.

At independence the assimilated Africans—*assimilados*—constituted less than 1 percent of Angolan Africans, while over 95 percent could neither read nor write. The *assimilados* occupied

Although they have preserved much of their traditional culture, some Mbundu, particularly those in urban areas, have also adapted to modern Angolan society. Seen here are a group of Mbundu schoolchildren in Moçamedes.

important social and administrative positions. Therefore, some of them had been used to promote colonial culture.

The *assimilados* have generally been criticized as an African elite who lost touch with their own culture and people. However, neither the Mbundu *assimilados* nor those from other parts of Angola absorbed Portuguese culture entirely. Rather, they accepted some aspects of Portuguese culture while still being rooted firmly in their own culture. It was the *assimilados* who initiated and promoted intellectual and armed resistance against the Portuguese.

In the 1950s Neto, along with other *assimilados,* founded the Center for African Studies in Luanda. The literature issued by the

Center helped greatly to revive interest in African culture and African history.

The Mbundu, like other Angolans, have preserved much of their culture. They have also shown their ability to use new ideas to benefit themselves. Arranged marriages still happen, and the bride's parents receive a payment of cattle from the groom's family. Fertility ceremonies are still held in Mbundu villages. Matrilineal relations are highly respected in the villages, but the bonds are much weaker in the urban centers.

Most Mbundu women continue to perform the traditional chores of homemaking and childbearing. Marriage outside the lineage group is still preferred, but the traditional rules governing relations between the sexes are easily ignored in the urban centers.

The present Angolan government strongly encourages all Angolans to celebrate their cultural roots. It sponsors traditional festivals, dances, and music. It also realizes the need to modernize some traditional norms and practices that are inappropriate for a multiethnic population. It campaigns against belief in witchcraft and discrimination against women. Because of the number of indigenous languages in Angola, Portuguese remains the national language.

▼ CONCLUSION ▼
The Mbundu have a history that dates back

to antiquity. It reaches beyond the recall of oral histories and written documents. The lack of firm data has meant that many gaps exist in our knowledge of the rich past of the Mbundu.

Within the limits of the technology available to them, the Mbundu have adapted admirably to their environment and to changing times and demands. Through interaction with others they have acquired and communicated new ideas and skills.

The arrival of the Portuguese in Angola posed an enormous threat to the Mbundu. The superior military force of the invaders finally led to the defeat and colonization of the Angolan people. But the Mbundu coped with and adapted to this difficult period. The Mbundu survived Portuguese colonial rule with a strong sense of self-identity. This is a tribute to the strength and adaptability of Mbundu culture.▲

Glossary

El Dorado Imaginary country rich with gold; place of great abundance.

hango Title of Libolo king.

hinterland Region inland from the coast which supplies resources to a larger center.

Kimbundu Language of the Mbundu.

lunga (plural: *malunga*) Mbundu authority symbol carved in wood and associated with rain and agriculture.

matrilineal Relating to kinship with emphasis on the mother's line of descent.

mbinda (plural: *jimbinda*) Master-hunter.

nganga (plural: *jinganga*) Traditional healer or diviner who communicates with the spirit world.

ngola (plural: *angola*) Authority symbol associated with iron; title of Ndongo king.

ngundu (plural: *jingundu*) Mbundu lineage-village.

pemba Sacred powder applied by the Mbundu to promote female fertility.

polygyny Marriage to more than one wife.

pombeiros Portuguese traders.

transhumance Seasonal movement of livestock.

vunga (plural: *mavunga*) Title in the Libolo Kingdom.

For Further Reading

Ennis, Merlin. *Umbundu Folktales from Angola.*
Boston: Beacon Press, 1962.

Challenging Reading

Bender, Gerald J. *Angola Under the Portuguese,
the Myth and the Reality.* Los Angeles: University of California Press, 1978.

Birmingham, David. *Trade and Conflict in Angola.*
Oxford, UK: Clarendon Press, 1966.

Birmingham, David, and Phyllis M. Martin, eds.
History of Central Africa. White Plains, NY:
Longman Publishing Group, 1984.

Davidson, Basil. *In the Eye of the Storm: Angola's
People.* New York: Doubleday, 1972.

Martin, Phyllis M., and Patrick O'Meara, eds.
Africa, 2nd ed. Bloomington: Indiana
University Press, 1986.

Needham, D. E. *From Iron Age to Independence:
A History of Central Africa.* White Plains, NY:
Longman Publishing Group, 1985.

Shillington, Kevin. *History of Africa.* New York:
St. Martin's Press, 1995.

Wheeler, Douglas, and Rene Pelissier. *Angola.*
Westport, CT: Greenwood Press, 1978.

Index

ACKNOWLEDGEMENTS
The publisher wishes to thank Manuel Jordán, Ph.D. This volume
benefited greatly from both his knowledge of the cultures of the Mbundu
and neighboring peoples and his fieldwork photographs of the region.

ABOUT THE AUTHOR
Onwuka N. Njoku, Ph.D. currently teaches in the History Department
of the University of Nigeria at Nsukka.

PHOTO CREDITS Cover, pp. 8, 18, 20, 28, 29, 30, 37, 38, 53, 57 ©
Manuel Jordán, Ph.D.; p. 13 courtesy of The Stanley Collection, The
University of Iowa Museum of Art; pp. 22, 33 courtesy of The Birming-
ham Museum of Art, Alabama; pp. 44, 46, 58 © Elizabeth Ann
Schneider, Ph.D.

CONSULTING EDITOR Gary N. van Wyk, Ph.D.
LAYOUT AND DESIGN Kim Sonsky